Wildfires

Georgia Beth

Consultants

Alison Cawood
Director of Public Engagement
Smithsonian Environmental Research Center

Cheryl Lane, M.Ed.
Seventh Grade Science Teacher
Chino Valley Unified School District

Michelle Wertman, M.S.Ed.
Literacy Specialist
New York City Public Schools

Publishing Credits

Rachelle Cracchiolo, M.S.Ed., *Publisher*
Emily R. Smith, M.A.Ed., *SVP of Content Development*
Véronique Bos, *VP of Creative*
Dani Neiley, *Editor*
Robin Erickson, *Senior Art Director*
Kevin Pham, *Senior Graphic Designer*

Smithsonian Enterprises

Avery Naughton, *Licensing Coordinator*
Paige Towler, *Editorial Lead*
Jill Corcoran, *Senior Director, Licensed Publishing*
Brigid Ferraro, *Vice President of New Business and Licensing*
Carol LeBlanc, *President*

Image Credits: p.10 Cecilio Ricardo/USDA Forest Service; p.11 Darin Oswaldo/Getty Images; p.13 Signal Photos/Alamy Stock Photo; p.14 Josh Edelson/Getty Images; p.15 Patrick T. Fallon/Getty Images; p.15 Cole Burston/Getty Images; p.17 Andrew Avitt/USDA Forest Service; p.18 Brent Johnson/ NPS; p.19 Peter DaSilva/Alamy Stock Photo; p.20 Shay Levy/Alamy Stock Photo; p.21 Gina Rodgers/Alamy Stock Photo; p.22 Steve Cukrov/Shutterstock; p.25 Peter DaSilva/Alamy Stock Photo; p.26 Y. Matsui/NPS; all other images from iStock and/or Shutterstock

Library of Congress Cataloging in Publication Control Number: 2024030534

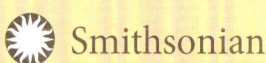

5482 Argosy Avenue
Huntington Beach, CA 92649
www.tcmpub.com
ISBN 979-8-7659-6875-8
© 2025 Teacher Created Materials, Inc.
Printed by: 51497
Printed in: China

Table of Contents

Inside a Wildfire

A fiery **inferno** burns out of control, spreading breathtakingly fast. Orange and red flames flicker and dance. The air is scorching hot with the temperature measuring over 1,093 °C (2,000 °F). Animals flee, and humans **evacuate**. Homes burn to the ground. Thousands of trees turn into ash and charcoal. This is what a wildfire looks like. And wildfires are becoming more common as our climate changes.

In the United States alone, two million hectares (five million acres) of land are affected by wildfires each year. Wildfires are most common in areas with trees and **brush** where there are droughts, or periods of little rain. Hot, dry conditions make it easier for fires to start and spread.

a wildfire at night

Wildfires destroy the glass and plastics in cars, leaving behind only ruined metal.

Wildfires affect humans, animals, and plants. Wildfire smoke is a health hazard that lowers air quality and irritates people's lungs. Wildfires destroy homes, vegetation, and habitats for animals. They can affect sources of drinking water and even cause death. During wildfires, entire ecosystems can be affected.

Wildfires have occurred on our planet throughout time. Learning about the chemistry of wildfires helps firefighters know how to stop them and create planned fires that have some surprising benefits. Plus, knowing the risks and effects of wildfires allows people to prepare for them, predict them, and stay safe from them.

Large wildfires can be seen from space.

Fire Chemistry

Every fire needs three essential ingredients to start **combustion**: fuel, oxygen, and heat. These ingredients make up a model called the *fire triangle*. If any of these ingredients are missing, a fire cannot burn.

In wildfires, fuel can include tree resin, vegetation, dry grasses, leaves, litter, or anything that burns. The next ingredient, oxygen, is found in the air. The air we breathe is made up of 21 percent oxygen, and a fire only needs 16 percent oxygen in the air to start. The final ingredient is heat. Sometimes, it comes from a natural source, such as lightning. Other times, heat comes from a human-made source. Campfires, cigarettes, fireworks, damaged power lines, and **arson** have all sparked wildfires. When these three ingredients come together, a wildfire can **ignite**.

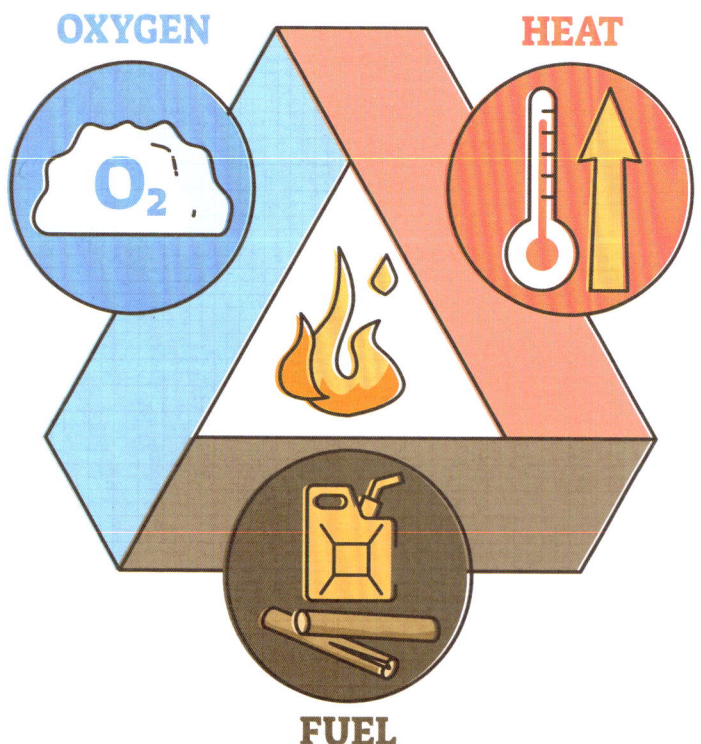

A Closer Look

You may have seen a small campfire or candle flame before. The same flames that occur in those small fires can be seen in large-scale wildfires, too. In a wildfire, flames destroy trees and break them down. A fire's temperature and the chemical makeup of the trees determine how much of the wood burns and how much turns to **char** or ash. The parts that burn turn into gases or smoke. The parts that turn into char form a solid black substance, and the parts that turn into ash become powdery and gray.

FUN FACT

The color of a fire's flames depends on the fuel source and temperature. Wildfire flames are usually red, orange, or yellow. The color of a fire's smoke also depends on the fuel source. Black smoke is caused by burning plastic or rubber. Lighter gray or white smoke is caused by burning wood and straw.

Exothermic Reaction

Even though wildfires destroy trees and homes, they do not destroy energy. Instead, they transform energy. Wildfires are the effect of a chemical reaction called an *exothermic reaction*. In this process, substances that burn react together. They release energy as heat and light. This is why you can warm your hands by a fire or see a campfire lighting up a campsite.

During this reaction, fuel and oxygen act as **reactants**. Flames heat the fuel and break down molecules inside. Complex gases made of hydrogen, carbon, and oxygen are burned. These molecules break down into atoms. Then, different molecules form and emerge in the flames. Carbon dioxide and water are the **products**. This is an intense, complex process.

Combustion Reaction

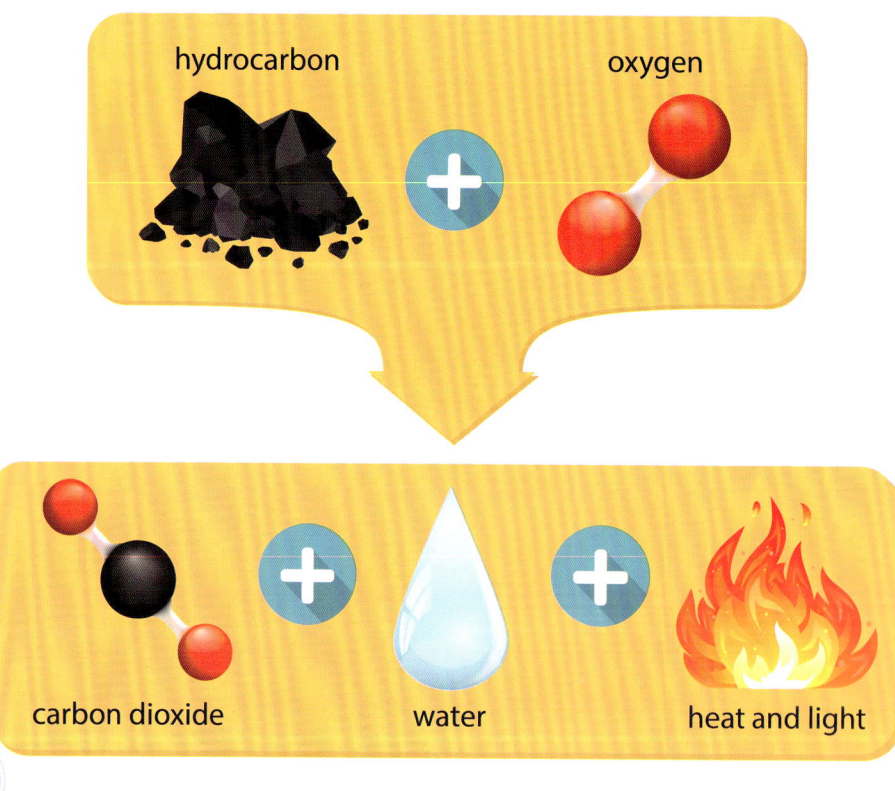

hydrocarbon   oxygen

carbon dioxide   water   heat and light

Emissions produced by a wildfire depend on the type of fuel burned. For example, savanna grasslands tend to produce large amounts of black carbon. Trees in fresh, green forests produce ammonia and nitrogen dioxide when they burn. **Peatland** fires can burn underground and produce methane and carbon monoxide. In large quantities, all these emissions are harmful to the environment.

smoke and flames from a peatland fire

Environmental Conditions

Because wildfires produce heat, they can burn for a long time if their fuel and oxygen sources are uninterrupted. Weather conditions, such as wind or high temperatures, can make wildfires more severe.

A climate feedback loop exists with wildfires. Climate change creates longer fire seasons during months when air is warm and dry. And longer fire seasons put more harmful emissions like carbon dioxide into the air, speeding up the rate of climate change.

Stopping Wildfires

When a wildfire breaks out, the fire triangle reminds firefighters of what's important. Reducing the fuel, oxygen, and heat sources for a fire is their goal. Firefighters also work to reach 100 percent containment of a fire. They create a **perimeter** around the fire, keeping it from spreading farther. Stopping a fire requires years of training, teamwork, and dedication. Over 70,000 wildfires break out around the world each year. When they do, firefighters move quickly.

Members of a hotshot crew spray water on the ground, ensuring that no hot coals remain.

On the scene of a wildfire, firefighters work in crews. First, the helitack crew uses helicopters to transport supplies and firefighters to the site. Helicopters can also drop water or fire **retardant**, which slows the fire. Next, the hotshot crew works on the ground. This crew works on the most challenging parts of a fire. They use bulldozers and chain saws to clear brush or trees, removing a fire's major fuel sources. These firefighters typically spend long periods away from their homes, fighting the fire night and day. Then, the people who hike into the fire are the hand crew. They rely on smaller hand tools, such

as axes and shovels, to cut away fuel and **smother** flames. They dig up roots and clear brush until only dirt remains. Finally, the engine crew carries in water or firefighting foam in special fire engines. They use hoses and pumps to spray water or foam onto the fire to reduce the heat.

FUN FACT

Smoke jumpers may be called to the scene of a wildfire when it first breaks out. These specially trained firefighters take a plane or helicopter to the area. Then, they use parachutes to jump down to the source of the flames. They work quickly to stop wildfires from spreading.

Equipment

Firefighters wear special gear to stay safe. Helmets protect their heads from falling debris. Sometimes, a helmet will have a **shroud** attached to it. This protects their skin from smoke and heat. Face masks filter out dangerous chemicals and provide clean air for breathing. Fire-resistant clothing and gloves protect their bodies from the extreme heat. Durable boots help them hike across rough **terrain**. Finally, firefighters may wear goggles, sunglasses, and ear protectors to keep their eyes and ears safe.

Special tools help firefighters do their difficult work. Flares burn away vegetation to create containment lines. Portable water pumps allow firefighters to carry water to areas that are hard to reach. Smaller items, such as compasses or whistles, may be carried in their backpacks. Compasses help them know which direction a fire is heading, and whistles can be used to signal for help. A variety of weather instruments help firefighters measure wind and temperature conditions.

helmet

backpack with **SCBA**

fire-resistant clothing

fire-resistant gloves

flares

compass

durable boots

Drones with special thermal cameras can be flown over a wildfire to find hot spots.

New Developments

Fire experts work on developing new tools and techniques to fight fires. They might test new materials for tents and clothing, develop new tools, and enhance vehicles. They consider how technology, such as drones, can be used to observe fires from a safe distance. Even the smallest changes can make a big difference. For example, some wildfire trucks have been painted green instead of red. The color change makes them easier to see in smoky, dark conditions.

ENGINEERING

A Safe Place

Wildfires can change direction rapidly due to winds. If firefighters get trapped by a fire's sudden movement, they can use special tents called *fire shelters* to protect themselves. These tents look like long, silvery domes. They are designed to protect firefighters from flames and the heat of a fire.

Historic Wildfires

In North America, wildfires have become increasingly severe in past decades. Here are just a few of the record-breaking wildfires. In each case, strong winds and dry conditions caused the flames to burn out of control.

The Camp Fire, 2018

California is no stranger to wildfires. The state gets very dry and hot in the summer months. But when an electrical line failed in Northern California, it sparked and ignited a record-breaking wildfire. Wind helped the flames spread rapidly, destroying most of the buildings in several towns. At the time, this was the deadliest fire in the state since 1933. A total of 85 people died. It was also the most expensive natural disaster in the world that year. It caused billions of dollars in damage.

More than 18,000 structures were destroyed in the Camp Fire.

Hospital patients were evacuated during the Camp Fire.

the aftermath of the wildfire in Lahaina

Lahaina Wildfire, 2023

On the island of Maui in Hawai'i, the coastal town of Lahaina experienced the deadliest fire in state history in 2023. A brush fire caused by a fallen power line was worsened by winds. The flames quickly spread into neighborhoods and began destroying homes. Residents had to evacuate with little notice. Roads became jammed as the fire surged through the main part of town. Some people who survived the fire had to jump into the ocean to avoid the flames. In the end, this fire took the lives of more than 100 people.

MATHEMATICS

The Cost of Fire

Between March and November 2023, numerous wildfires broke out in Canada. This wildfire season broke the country's record for the most area burned. It was also the most expensive. Fires caused millions of dollars in damages to people's homes and property. The government also spent millions of dollars on resources to fight the fires.

Thousands of homes burned during Canada's 2023 wildfire season.

Controlled Burns

It may be hard to think of any benefits to wildfires, but they are a natural part of many ecosystems. Controlled burns, also known as planned fires, can stimulate new plant growth and prevent catastrophic blazes. The U.S. Forest Service and other government land management agencies complete controlled burns every year.

Every controlled burn follows a mindful plan. Fire managers decide what the fire's purpose will be, how big it will be, and if the weather conditions are right. They also create a plan to tell the public about the fire so people are not alarmed when they see smoke. They keep firefighting resources nearby in case the fire begins to burn out of control. But because of the careful planning, this is very rare.

Firefighters in California conduct a controlled burn.

Pile burns are controlled burns of collected wood, brush, and other material.

There are several reasons why a controlled burn may happen. For instance, if there are too many tall trees in a forest, the forest floor doesn't get enough sun for **saplings** to grow. When fire is used to burn away some trees, it makes space for the sun to shine through. Another reason is to prevent hazardous fuel, such as dry brush, from building up. Also, fires add carbon to the ground, creating rich soil for new plants to grow in. The heat from fires can cause certain pine cones to release their seeds, encouraging new growth.

Indigenous Burns

For thousands of years, **Indigenous** peoples used controlled burns to care for their land. Their controlled burns cleared land for crops, hunting, and travel. Other times, controlled burns were used to herd animals, such as bison.

In the twentieth century, the U.S. government stopped Indigenous peoples from setting controlled burns. This resulted in the build-up of vegetation, increasing the risk of large wildfires. It was not a healthy time for forests or people. Today, that has changed. Indigenous peoples and government agencies work together to manage controlled burns. They also work with local organizations to share equipment, labor, and knowledge.

Members of the Southern Sierra Miwuk nation complete a traditional ceremony before California firefighters work on a controlled burn.

Different patterns, such as these stripes, can be used for controlled burns.

During Indigenous controlled burns, experts must follow four rules. First, they choose the right time for a burn. Season, temperature, weather, and time of day are all important factors. Second, they select the right place for a burn. Understanding the ecosystem and how the plants, animals, and landscape are related is crucial. This allows experts to determine where to start a fire and how big it should be. They might also plan escape routes for animals. Third, they protect personal rights and safety. They make sure that the burn plan does not negatively affect any people living on the land. The next generation that will live on and protect the land is also consulted. Finally, they decide whether a controlled burn is being done for the right reasons. For example, a controlled burn may be set to encourage plant variety when the vegetation begins to grow back. Through the entire process, Indigenous controlled burns aim to protect culture and manage resources.

Living with Wildfires

Because of the climate feedback loop, wildfires are here to stay. That's why fire experts do as much as they can to predict and prevent wildfires. With prediction, prevention, and safety techniques in mind, fire experts do their best to protect people from wildfires.

Predicting Wildfires

Not every wildfire can be prevented, but firefighters and fire experts can predict where wildfires might occur. They can direct resources to those areas as a way of preparation.

That gives firefighters a better chance at stopping fires before they burn out of control.

To see where fires may start, firefighters examine the **topography** and ecology of the areas they serve. They examine several factors, including weather, wind patterns, and dryness levels. They learn how different types of trees burn, and they look at how much dead wood or brush is in an area. That allows them to understand how much available fuel exists. Firefighters also study the slope of the land because fire burns faster uphill than downhill. They consider whether a fire is more likely to spread quickly in certain areas.

Firefighters work together to predict where a fire may travel.

All these factors lead back to the three elements of the fire triangle. Firefighters know that oxygen in the air is a constant. But they can study what fuel is available. They can learn what **variables** might increase or decrease heat. With these studies, they can predict which areas are at risk for wildfires.

TECHNOLOGY

Recognizing Fire with AI

AI, or artificial intelligence, can help recognize signs of wildfires. AI systems pair with video feeds from mountaintop lookouts. The AI is trained to spot signs of smoke in these videos. When smoke is spotted, local fire managers are notified.

fire danger sign in
Sedona, Arizona

National Fire Danger Rating System

The National Fire Danger Rating System is run by the U.S. Forest Service. This system tells how likely a wildfire is to occur at a given time and place. It takes several factors into account. These include weather forecasts, terrain, and types of available fuel. This system also looks at how much energy the fire might release. Then, it determines the risk of a fire igniting and spreading. A rating of 0 to 100 is given to show the chance of a fire igniting. So, on a rainy day, the risk of ignition might be 0. On a dry day with lightning forecasted, the risk might be 75.

ARTS

Smokey Bear

The U.S. Forest Service created Smokey Bear in 1944. This cartoon bear is a mascot for fire prevention. You may have seen him on forest signs before! His image is still used to teach the public about fire prevention.

The five levels of fire danger are shown on this sign.

This valuable information is not just shared among firefighters. The U.S. Forest Service communicates as much information as possible to the public. One way they do this is through rating the potential for wildfires. Five color-coded levels are used to rate the risk of fire danger. National forests have road signs that show the current fire danger rating. This information is also provided online. The first level on this scale is the low, or green-colored, rating. At this level, there is a low risk of wildfires starting. Controlled burns typically happen at this level. Then, the levels continue to moderate, high, very high, and extreme. At this last red-colored level, wildfires can start and spread rapidly. Fire managers may decide to close national forests to the public or put temporary bans on campfires.

Staying Safe

Every year, wildfires destroy ecosystems and homes. Communities all over the world can be affected. Even if you do not live in an area that is at risk of wildfires, knowing how to prepare for any type of fire is important. Preparation can help keep people safe.

Wildfire Safety

People who live in areas where wildfires happen typically have safety plans in place. This allows them to prepare for how they will leave if they must evacuate. They may have packed bags with water, food, clothes, medicine, and important documents. They might keep pet carriers near their supplies so everything they need stays in one place. People with larger animals, such as horses, make sure that their transportation is part of their safety plan. And during wildfire season, they clear dry brush and other fuel away from the outsides of their homes. They also make sure that their smoke detectors are working.

When people evacuate from a wildfire, they typically fit everything they can into their cars and go to an evacuation center.

When a wildfire breaks out, people at risk move quickly. They close the windows and vents in their homes to stop smoke from getting in. They might spray their houses with water to prevent them from burning. If the fire is close to them, they will check the news online for evacuation instructions and official reports. They might also check on their neighbors and offer help before they leave. Finally, wearing masks protects their lungs from toxins in the air.

FUN FACT

Fire extinguishers and fire blankets are useful fire safety tools people can purchase for their homes. Fire extinguishers can be used to spray fire retardant on small fires. Fire blankets are made of flameproof materials, and they can be used to smother small fires.

The Power of Fire

Fire has been with us for thousands of years. The earliest humans used it as a source of heat, a method of cooking, and a form of protection. Fire could also be used as a place to gather. Throughout time, fire has always been an essential part of life and survival for humans.

Fire still actively shapes our lives, but in new and different ways. Large-scale wildfires play a role in climate change, producing dramatic changes on Earth. And wildfires are often the result of human activity. It creates a feedback loop, with fire sparking more fire.

A firefighter stands in the remains of a forest after a wildfire.

Wherever there are forests, grasslands, or shrubs, there is fire. With over 70,000 fires breaking out each year around the world, nearly everyone will be affected by a wildfire in some way. People may experience a wildfire's destruction or have to evacuate their homes due to the risk of a wildfire. Or, they may experience a lack of resources or poor health because of wildfires.

Humans have found many ways to predict and prevent wildfires. Technology and fire rating systems help firefighters study areas of concern. Controlled burns can stop larger wildfires from breaking out. And people can learn about fire safety to keep themselves and their homes safe. Learning about wildfires allows us to live with them and lessen their effects.

STEAM CHALLENGE

Define the Problem

Fire safety is not just limited to wildfires—it's important to keep yourself safe from fire danger in the kitchen. One challenge is preventing burns from the handles of hot pots and pans. Cookware manufacturers are seeking design ideas from engineers for innovative pot and pan grips. They want to prevent the handle of a pot or pan from getting too hot while still allowing food to cook inside. Your task is to create a pot or pan grip that will slow or stop the transfer of heat energy to protect your hands.

 **Constraints:** You may only use the materials that are provided to you.

 **Criteria:** Your pan grip must fit over the handle of a cooking pot or pan. It should also maintain room temperature after exposure to a heat source.

Research and Brainstorm

How do conduction, convection, and radiation work in the kitchen when cooking? What is the difference between exothermic and endothermic reactions? How can this information help you create a design that protects peoples' hands?

Design and Build

Sketch two or more designs for your pan grip. Label the parts of your grip, and include labels for the materials that you intend to use. Work with a partner to share your ideas. Together, decide on one final design, and build a model to test.

Test and Improve

Rest a thermometer on top of your grip (or scan with an infrared thermometer) to gather baseline data. Record this temperature. Then, place your grip on a preheated hot pad or hot plate for several minutes. Test and record the temperature at various increments. Did the grip stop the transfer of heat energy? How can you modify your design to better protect a user's hands? Make modifications and retest, reassessing how well it meets the criteria.

Reflect and Share

What part of the STEAM Challenge did you find the most interesting? What problems did you face, and how did you resolve them? What properties of your chosen materials allowed for success? Why might manufacturers struggle to make pan grips that can be universally used in an oven, on a stove, and in a microwave?

29

Glossary

arson—the illegal act of starting a harmful fire on purpose

brush—shrubs and low grasses that cover the ground in certain areas

char—material that has turned into charcoal or carbon

combustion—the act of burning; a chemical process that produces heat and light

emissions—substances put into the air

evacuate—to leave a place in an organized way, especially for protection

ignite—to catch fire

Indigenous—of or relating to the earliest known people to live in a place

inferno—an intense fire

peatland—marshy or damp land made of peat, or organic matter from decaying plants

perimeter—a continuous line that forms a boundary around an area

products—resulting substances or outputs of chemical reactions

reactants—substances that undergo and are changed by chemical reactions

retardant—a substance that prevents or stops something, especially the outbreak of fire

saplings—young trees

SCBA—self-contained breathing apparatus, which contains a supply of breathable air for use in very smoky conditions

shroud—something that covers, screens, or guards, such as a cloth face mask for firefighting

smother—to put out a fire by removing oxygen

terrain—the physical features of an area of land

topography—the shape, height, and depth of the features of a place

variables—factors in scientific experiments or mathematical equations

Index

CAREER ADVICE
from Smithsonian

Do you want to have a career in environmental science?

Here are some tips to keep in mind for the future.

"Embrace your curiosity and ask questions about everything!"

–Dr. Katrina Lohan, Coastal Disease Ecologist, Smithsonian Environmental Research Center

"Joining environmental or green clubs and volunteering with similar kinds of organizations can be a great way to learn and meet other people who are also interested in environmental science."

– Dr. Alison Cawood, Director of Public Engagement, Smithsonian Environmental Research Center